SUGAR BABY

by Alan Harris

Sugar Baby was first produced by Dirty Protest as part of Wales in Edinburgh with the support of Chapter, the Arts Council of Wales, Wales Arts International and British Council Wales.

It was first performed on 4 August 2017 in Paines Plough's Roundabout @ Summerhall, at Edinburgh Festival Fringe 2017.

It was revived on 1 August 2018 in Paines Plough's Roundabout @ Summerhall, at Edinburgh Festival Fringe 2018.

CYMRU YNG NGHAEREDIN
WALES IN EDINBURGH

Cyngor Celfyddydau Cymru
Arts Council of Wales

wales arts international
celfyddydau rhyngwladol cymru

ARIENNIR GAN
Y LOTERI
LOTTERY FUNDED

Sugar Baby

by Alan Harris

Cast

Adam Redmore

Creative Team

Director	Catherine Paskell
Lighting Designer	Ace McCarron
Sound Designer	Dan Lawrence
Assistant Producer	Glesni Price-Jones
Stage Manager	Dave Beever
Marketing Consultant	Rhian Lewis
Press and PR	Catrin Rogers
	(The Corner Shop PR Wales)
Cover Illustration	Nic Finch

Dirty Protest

Matthew Bulgo
Branwen Davies
Angela Harris
Claire Hill
Catherine Paskell
Tim Price

Dirty Protest Theatre Ltd: registered in England and Wales 10584406
dirtyprotesttheatre.co.uk
info@dirtyprotesttheatre.co.uk
Twitter: @DirtyProtest
Facebook: @DirtyProtestTheatre
Instagram: @DirtyProtestTheatre

This production has been licensed by arrangement with The Agency
(London) Ltd, 24 Pottery Lane, London W11 4LZ, info@theagency.co.uk

Cast

ADAM REDMORE
Theatre credits: *Wonderman* (Gagglebabble/National Theatre Wales); *Roberto Zucco* (Chapter Arts); *Maudie's Rooms* (Sherman Cymru); *Milked* (Pentabus Theatre); *Tonypandemonium* (National Theatre Wales); *Caligula* (Chapter Arts); *Clytemnestra* (Sherman Theatre); *Serious Money* (Waking Exploits); *Double Falsehood* (The Union Theatre); *Helianthus* and *Squat Show 1* (The Squat Collective); *Doctor Faustus/School for Scandal* (Greenwich Theatre); *Follow* (Finborough Theatre).

Television credits: *Doctors*, *Silent Witness* and *The Bill*.

Radio credits: *Devil's Violin* (BBC Radio Drama) and *If You're Reading This* (BBC Radio 4).

Creative Team

ALAN HARRIS | WRITER

Plays include: *For All I Care* (National Theatre Wales NHS70); *How My Light Is Spent* (Royal Exchange, Manchester/Sherman/ Theatre by the Lake; Bruntwood Judges' Prize 2015); *Love, Lies and Taxidermy* (Paines Plough/ Sherman/Theatr Clwyd); *The Opportunity of Efficiency* (New National Theatre Tokyo/National Theatre Wales); *The Magic Toyshop* (Invisible Ink/Theatr Iolo); *The Future For Beginners* (liveartshow/ Wales Millennium Centre); *A Good Night Out in the Valleys* (National Theatre Wales); *A Scythe of Time* (New York Musical Theatre Festival); *Cardboard Dad* (Sherman); *Orange* (Sgript Cymru). He has also written radio plays for BBC Radio 4 and Radio 3.

Libretti include: *Marsha: A Girl Who Does Bad Things* (liveartshow/Arcola Grimeborn Festival); *The Hidden Valley* (Birdsong Opera/Welsh National Opera/Tête à Tête); *The Journey* (Welsh National Opera); *Rhinegold, Manga Sister* (both liveartshow/The Yard, London).

CATHERINE PASKELL | DIRECTOR

Catherine is Artistic Director of Dirty Protest and an independent performance director from Cardiff. Previous to this she was a founding Creative Associate of National Theatre Wales.

Catherine trained on the Theatre Directing MFA at Birkbeck, University of London and was resident director at Contact, Manchester and Octagon Theatre Bolton.

Directing credits include: a new production of Shakespeare's *The Merchant of Venice* adapted into Portuguese, for the Centro Cultural Banco do Brasil, Belo Horizonte (People's Palace Projects/British Council); *Parallel Lines* (Dirty Protest, Chapter Cardiff/tour); *The Beach* (Hide&Seek/National Theatre Wales); *An Audience with Jeff Goldblum* (The Junket Club/Edinburgh Festival Fringe); *Top of the Hour* (BBC Radio Wales); *Drama Queen* (Unity Theatre, Liverpool); *White People* (Theatre503); *Top Bunk* (Oldham Coliseum); *When the Lights Went Out* (Tara Arts national tour); *Be the Hunter* (Soho Theatre).

Catherine's production of *Parallel Lines* for Dirty Protest won Best Production in the English Language at the Theatre Critics of Wales Awards.

She is a Fellow of the Clore Leadership Programme and the RSA.

ACE McCARRON | LIGHTING DESIGNER

Ace McCarron has been a freelance lighting designer since leaving the Royal Court Theatre in 1988. He has enjoyed a long experience with Music Theatre Wales and with The Wrestling School, a company formed to produce the plays of Howard Barker. Most of Ace's work is with contemporary theatre and opera and he has designed lighting for companies such as Paines Plough, Shared Experience, the Bush Theatre, the Traverse, the Tricycle, the Almeida, Theatr Genedlaethol Cymru, the Sherman, Scottish Opera, Muziektheater Transparant, Operastudio Vlaanderen, the Royal Opera House Garden Venture and many more. Along with composer Guy Harries, Ace won the inaugural 'Flourish' award for an adaptation of Marina Lewycka's novel *Two Caravans*.

DAN LAWRENCE | SOUND DESIGNER

Dan was raised in Aberystwyth and went on to study Pop Music and Recording in Salford, graduating in 1992. He has lived in Cardiff since 2003 and has worked as a composer, musical director and sound designer with many Welsh theatre companies including National Theatre Wales (*A Good Night Out in the Valleys, De Gabay, Mother Courage*) and Theatr Genedlaethol Cymru (*Y Storm, Y Negesydd, Y Fenyw Ddaeth o'r Môr*), Sherman Cymru (*Ho Ho Ho, Pinocchio, The Elves & the Shoemakers, The Princess & the Pea, The Emperor's New Clothes*), Theatr Iolo, Taking Flight Theatre, Hijinx, Gagglebabble, West Yorkshire Playhouse and Dirty Protest.

Dan also runs his own recording studio in Cardiff, tutors young bands and continues to perform regularly with the traditional Welsh folk duo Olion Byw, and the Welsh/Galician collaboration band Maelog.

GLESNI PRICE-JONES | ASSISTANT PRODUCER

Glesni is a freelance producer working with many of the most exciting production companies in Wales. Previously, Glesni worked as a Stage and Production Manager with National Theatre Wales, Theatr Genedlaethol, yello brick, August 012, Neontopia and Sherman Theatre. Current projects include *Lovecraft (Not the Sex Shop in Cardiff)* (Carys Eleri and WMC); *Enough is Enough* (Be Aware Productions, UK tour); *Robinson: The Other Island, Give it a Name* (UK tour); *Saethu Cwningod/Shooting Rabbits* (PowderHouse, Theatre Genedlaethol Cymru, Sherman)

DAVE BEEVER | STAGE MANAGER

Dave studied Lighting Design & Production Management at Northbrook College, Sussex graduating in 2007 with a Foundation Degree.

Full-time employment has included The Courtyard, Hereford and The Corn Exchange, Newbury.

Freelance work has included Birmingham International Dance Festival, The Globe in the West End, too many EdFringe shows to mention and of course, the awesome *Sugar Baby*!

Dave is currently Technical Manager at Zoo Venues for Edinburgh Festival Fringe 2018 and is chuffed to bits as a Welsh boy to be back at the Fringe with Dirty Protest in ROUNDABOUT.

Dirty Protest

Dirty Protest is Wales' award-winning theatre company leading the development, promotion and production of new writing for performance.

Launched in 2007, the company has produced over 300 new plays by over 200 established and emerging writers, including Welsh writers Katherine Chandler, Gary Owen, Brad Birch, Alan Harris, Dafydd James, Ed Thomas, Kelly Jones, Tim Price, and Meredydd Barker, and British playwrights including Duncan Macmillan, Rebecca Lenkiewicz, James Graham, Joel Horwood, Chloe Moss, Lucy Kirkwood and Jack Thorne.

Dirty Protest stage new sell-out plays in theatres and alternative venues, from pubs and clubs, to music festivals, kebab shops, hairdressers and forests. Alongside full-length productions, Dirty Protest stage regular short-play nights where established and wannabe writers are presented on the same platform, providing opportunities for writers, directors and actors. These nights present a shot of theatrical tequila without the paraphernalia, all for the price of a pint.

Dirty Protest has worked with partners including the Royal Court Theatre, the Almeida Theatre, Traverse Edinburgh, Soho Theatre, Chapter Cardiff, Theatr Clwyd, Galeri Caernarfon, Camden Roundhouse, Wales Millennium Centre, Sherman Theatre, Latitude Festival, Festival No.6, and many more. Dirty Protest's annual new writing festival, 'Dirty, Gifted & Welsh' is produced in partnership with National Theatre Wales.

In December 2016, Dirty Protest produced the hit one-man show *Last Christmas* by Matthew Bulgo at the Traverse Theatre in Edinburgh. This followed an acclaimed run at the 2014 Edinburgh Festival Fringe, with a five-star review from *The Scotsman*, and a transfer to Soho Theatre.

> ★★★★★ 'There's a real humanity to *Last Christmas*, a truth in the writing and playing that makes it one of the best things on the Fringe this year. Don't miss it' (*The Scotsman*).

Dirty Protest also won Best Production in the English Language at the Theatre Critics of Wales Awards for the premiere of Katherine Chandler's *Parallel Lines* (Wales Drama Award, Susan Smith Blackburn Prize Finalist).

> '*Parallel Lines* is a significant production in the history of Welsh theatre' (*British Theatre Guide*).

Acclaim for *Sugar Baby*

'Nobody writes more sweetly or with such comic compassion about low-life than Alan Harris'

Lyn Gardner in the *Guardian*

'The packed audience loves it' ★ ★ ★ ★ *The Times*

'Theatrical tour de force' ★ ★ ★ ★ *The Scotsman*

'Stonking good fun' ★ ★ ★ ★ *The Stage*

Added to the British Council Showcase at Edinburgh Festival Fringe 2017 as a recommended show.

SUGAR BABY

Alan Harris

Note on Play

One actor plays all the characters.

Italics are for real-time dialogue.

Narrative dialogue is not in italics.

A dash on its own line (–) indicates a pause for thought.

This text went to press before the end of rehearsals and so may differ slightly from the play as performed.

Prologue

I try not to act on impulse.

But I can't help it.

Which, to be fair, is the problem with impulse.

Or the problem with me.

–

I'll start again.

I acted on impulse.

I was sitting on a bus stop waiting for the 61 minding my own when I sees a girl standing in the middle of Fairwater Road with a Beamer coming towards her.

I gets up, sprints the six yards and grabs her out of the road.

Impulse gets you into trouble.

The sort of trouble that leads to Vicci Park, murder, going on the run and Billy the Seal.

Seriously there's a seal in this story.

The thing that's always held me back is sharing – I've always hated it. Like when you're out and there's other people there and they say: shall we get something to share? No – I wants my own plate of food.

Sharing is dangerous ground.

I once told someone that once – once mind you – I played with a Wendy house with my cousin in Malpas, little Justine, and every times I sees him now they says, this person I told, they says 'How's it going, Wendy?'

I've always had a vision that I'm, like, some kind of lone wolf – I know.

And that I'm really in a movie – I'm the central character, obviously.

A'right, my story is a bit crappy and dirty and set in Fairwater and not LA and I feels a bit of a bell-end because people like me are not supposed to have a story.

But, anyway, that's a load of shit.

What I want to tell you about is what happened on August 18th last year.

The story, really, starts before I save a girl from being run over by a Beamer.

About thirty-seven minutes before.

I'm sitting in Oggy's.

Sweating.

Is not a bad day outside but he's got the heating cranked right up.

I'm sweating so much my bollocks is damp, you know?

Part One

I wants cash off Oggy.

Six thousand pounds to be exact.

As I sits in Oggy's front room –

The 'waiting room'.

The same thoughts come into my head:

Don't fuck this up.

Don't fuck this up.

As mantras go it's not a great one.

Not very positive.

I likes to think of myself as a positive guy.

That's why I grew a moustache.

Not a great moustache but there it is.

I felt it would distinguish me from the crowd.

Really.

It's 10.27 a.m.

I look up to see Gary in the doorway. Mo's behind as they both can't fit in the doorway together. Mo has to talk over Gary's shoulder:

A'right, sunshine, Oggy will see you now.

I works as a drug dealer in Fairwater.

It's a drugs cooperative.

There's six equal shares. Everyone grows separate and then pools the gear. Then if anyone gets arrested, no biggie. You gets done but you still get a sixth of the profits. You don't get as much cash as independents but it takes the risks out of the game. Makes sense yeah? I'm pulling down, most weeks, about two hundred quid. I know, not exactly Pablo Escobar but it keeps me going. Just.

I grows my gear behind Stannie's house. In a greenhouse.

I puts in fake tomatoes and no one's any the wiser. Serious. The price of toms has gone up recently which is a fucking blow.

Stannie is a little... shy, what with his actual job being a fence for stolen goods. If you wants it, Stannie can get it: from a labradoodle to a new passport to a mobility scooter. Serious.

After Celia (who you will meet later), left it was just me and my dad, Mark, living opposite Fairwater Fish Bar, you knows? The red-brick flats? Celia lived there till I was fourteen. If you go up the top of the road, you can see right over the city – see the Principality Stadium and down, beyond that Cardiff Bay. It's that close.

I don't call him Dad, I calls him Mark or 'the old man'. My dad Mark's 'Mark' is a traditional one with a 'K' and when him and Celia had me they thought they'd name their boy after Mark but give it a modern twist.

My 'Marc' is with a 'C'.

Tha's a modern twist in Fairwater.

Sitting in Oggy's front room I'm thinking:

Don't fuck this up.

Don't fuck this up.

Like my life depends on it.

Only it's not my life that depends on it.

It's Mark's.

With a 'K'.

Oggy is a twat.

A twat with cash.

He suffers from the desire that a lot of men round here suffers with – a desire to never be a disappointment to himself.

Recently there's been this thing about Wonga clamping down and for many it's a nightmare – you just can't get through the week to get food. And, believe it or not, Oggy's rates are actually cheaper than Wonga or Tangerine or whatever the fuck company. So there is a lie that loan sharks are exploitative.

There is also a stereotype that if you can't pay, loan sharks come round your house and fuck you up.

That bit is true.

Not Oggy personally – he couldn't punch his way out of a Clark's pie – but Gary and Mo would.

So I'm in Oggy's thinking:

Don't fuck this up and then it's my turn.

Oggy could have afforded a proper office but made his 'clients' come to his house; something about lording it over your fellow man, you know?

For some reason, I thinks that's why he's got the heating on on a nice day.

Oggy's taken the gangster thing to heart.

And is now playing his part.

He has a tattoo of him and Beyoncé in bed together, wrapped in silk sheets, on his neck. When he speaks the vein in his neck moves and Beyoncé starts to jiggle back and forth.

What a twat.

I goes through. Oggy's done the back room out like a quaint pub, complete with pool table.

He waves his pool cue at a bar stool where I perches like a parrot with one leg.

Fucking shaky.

When I goes to speak – I just got to ask him why the heating's on – Oggy stops me with an imperious wave of his cue.

How's it going, Wendy?

–

When we was in school, Marc was in all the top sets, wasn't you, Wendy?

Gary and Mo do the laugh-along thing, even though they must know he's a complete cockstain too.

Remember when we went to Rachel Patterson's party, brah?

Every time I meets Oggy it's the same stories – or a version of them.

Wendy here had the chance to fuck the very same Rachel Patterson and you know what he did?

Dramatic pause for Gary and Mo's benefit.

He came in his pants even before he got to stick it in her.

Did I mention he was a twat?

I gives Oggy my pitch – *I'll get straight into it as I knows you're a busy man*, blah blah fucking blah.

Oggy actually plays a few shots while he's pretending to think about the proposal and then stops and gives it the two-hands-on-the-edge-of-the-table-lean-forward-I'm-going-to-be-earnest shit.

He gives it a second before Beyoncé starts to move her ass.

You wants me to lend you six thousand pounds so you can give it to your old man so that he can pay back a debt that he already owes me?

In a fucking nutshell.

Are you insane? I'll be no better off.

I'll owe you instead of the old man owing you.

But I'll still be owed the same amount.

Can see he's grasped the concept...

I tells him I can see he's grasped the concept.

'Concept'? Learn that in the top sets, did you?

Technically it won't really make a difference to you –

Part of the thing that marks me out from the crowd, apart from a weak moustache, is that I likes to use words like 'concept' and 'technically'.

You can take your concept and technically fuck yourself with it, brah. You tell your old man that if he can't pay then he shouldn't send his

–

his turdball of a son to try and stall for him.

The teachers at Cantonian High School are partially to blame for Oggy's lack of linguistic skills – they really didn't try with him.

Look, Marky-Marc, you don't want to lend off me.

Why? Cos we're mates?

Don't flatter yourself, brah.

Come on, Oggy, we goes way back.

How you gonna pay it back?

I'm a drug dealer.

You're having a laugh. Six Gs? You always did think you was more than you was.

Come on, Oggy.

Trust me on this, brah – I has made my final decision. You'll thank me one day.

Before I can plead and beg, Oggy gives me his final word on the matter:

Now fuck off.

My old man used to have a proper job in the paint factory near Ely Bridge. I never understood what he did there but after that went tits-up, him and the old girl went tits-up and then he started to look for other sources of income. He stole all the front doors from a new housing estate near Leckwith and when someone made a joke that our place was all front doors – we had front doors leading to everywhere; bathrooms, bedrooms, the lot – someone overheard who knew the guy that owned the site – a property developer called Bunce – and they kicked the shit out of my old man.

I comes home late and there's no door on the front of the flat. There's no doors at all, no door to the old man's bedroom and even though it was dark in there I can see he's hurt – the way he's lying on the duvet, sort of unnatural. His face looks like a cartoon, puffed-up... made me think of Jim Carrey, you know, in some kind of fucked-up film role. I don't know exactly what happened that night, but I bet it's one the old man plays over and over again in his mind. He has always thought of himself as a wheeler-dealer – but he's a shit one and that's led to his present predicament with – and my visit to – Oggy.

He's a regular at the Ex Club and Fairwater Library.

He fucking loves it. Reading.

No shit.

Currently he's reading The Spy Who Loved Me by Ian Fleming.

I love my father.

I also loves Fairwater – friendliest people in Cardiff and the Fairwater Fish Bar is the best. They will fry anything for you. They once deep-fried a kitten for me.

–

Sorry, did I say kitten? I meant Kit Kat.

My old man has two weeks to pay back Oggy. Then the interest piles up, then... I don't think he can take another Jim Carrey moment. As I walks out of Oggy's waiting room I wonders how much Wonga has tightened up.

Too much for me.

I knows I only has one alternative – and it's a horrible one. I decide to put a final decision off for a bit, I've got to go up to Stannie's and check on the crop and on the way there I'll decide whether I make the trek over to Cyncoed to humiliate myself in pursuit of the six grand.

And then I sees her.

Lisa.

Lisa Short loves Marc Chapps.

Always has.

She sat behind me at registration at Cantonian.

Staring at my neck. I could fucking feel her eyes on the back of my neck every day for five years.

If you sits behind someone and stare at the back of their neck every week-day for five years you will fall in love with them – it's inevitable.

She wrote Lisa loves Marc on every exercise book she ever had and on every desk in the reg class. LS heart MC.

I even got in trouble for it!

Yeah, it's not me, Mrs Stapleton – Marc's a little obsessed with me, aren't you, Marc.

In school I'd always been... aware of Lisa but had always thought she was a bit of a nutter, you knows the type. She was nothing great to look at but now she's blossomed, while I was fantastic-looking at school but now, yeah, I've maybe not had as many vitamins as I should have...

A tables-turned sort of thing.

Before I'm able to say 'Hi, Lis, been ages, good to see you, what the fuck are you in this shithole for?' she's up and away and into Oggy's inner sanctum.

Part Two

I'm on the bus stop waiting for the 61.

The little red electronic letters reads four minutes. It's said four minutes for eighteen minutes.

Lisa comes out of Oggy's house.

I half sees her coming towards the bus stop and think: does she have to? I just wanna be left alone.

Sees her cross the road.

But she's stuck – it's as if she can't cross the white line.

Get out of the road.

Get out of the –

You knows what happens next but, honest, it was like, you know that bit in The Matrix when the universe goes a bit funny?

On Llandaff Road there's this glitch in The Matrix, there's a ripple that… ripples the world when I grabs her. Everything, including the air, is liquid.

Then we snaps back to real time:

Fucking hell, Lisa, what you playing at? You could have been… you know. You okay?

It's a stupid question to ask a crying girl but there you go.

Fuck, what did he do to you?

Yeah, hi, Marc?

I really wants to ignore her – if the 61 comes now I'm saved from speaking to her but the time's gone up, incredibly, to six minutes.

She's doing the crying thing but trying to keep it in.

Sobbing.

Making unnatural noises. Torture.

She hasn't even thanked me for saving her life!

I have enough shit of my own to deal with so I tries to hold back the flood of tears with:

Let me buy you a cuppa, yeah?

Isn't that what people are supposed to say in these situations?

Actually, Marc, I could do with a proper drink.

In the Ex Club, Lisa drank, rather surprisingly, cava.

There aren't many cava-drinkers in the Ex. They had to go to Spar next door to get a bottle.

I stick to the IPA – lower alcohol than SA, you never know what an afternoon like this will lead to.

After her third glass Lisa tells it. I doesn't want to hear it – got enough on my plate – but we're here now and the pints are sailing down my neck.

He wants what?

Pay off my debt little by little.

A – ?

Sugar baby.

Is like, what? A...

Paid girlfriend. Every time I goes out with him he'll knock a ton off my debt.

How much do you owe him?

Six grand.

Does everyone in Cardiff owe Oggy six grand?

Six grand? Fuck. That's a lot of time to spend with Oggy.

What choice do I have, Marc? – she tells me this as a fact, not a question.

And do you have to, you know? Fuck him?

That wasn't discussed but...

Everyone knows that Oggy is never going to get a woman like you so if you goes out with him everyone knows you're only with him cos he's paying you. What does that do for him?

Is what gangsters do.

I knows what Oggy dreams about when he settles into his king-size waterbed at night and pulls his black-satin sheets up around his scrawny fucking Beyoncé decorated neck and closes his eyes – he sees himself in a Jay-Z video.

I knew why Lisa had taken six Gs off Oggy – everyone in Fairwater knows, it was in the Echo, but that's a subject to avoid: sharing is not fucking caring.

Lisa finishes her glass of cava and does a little burp as the punters in the Ex say nothing to each other.

Basically, Lisa killed her mum. She'd taken her mum, who had some kind of weird wasting disease, to Switzerland to have her put down. And I fucking do not want to talk to her about that!

You want another, Marc? My shout.

I shouldn't... but why the fuck not?

Why people who wants to kill themselves just don't kill themselves I don't know – why drag their families into it? Why do people share the shit around?

I bought some nuts, Marc.

Right, I really do have to ditch her. I consider my options – if I go to the gents, can I fit through the window? But for some reason I say:

Fancy an ice cream, Lis?

They don't even have cava here, Marc.

Not here – maybe go down Vicci Park for a bit?

I'll buy the ice creams.

You promise?

Girl Guide's honour.

She didn't look like the Girl Guide sort.

Me and Lisa takes the 61 towards Vicci Park.

As we pass Eastern Avenue I sense an awkward question coming:

Why were you at Oggy's, Marc?

Do you think you're the only one in Fairwater capable of being a sugar baby?

No, serious, why?

My old man borrowed six grand off Oggy and bought a Transit full of knock-off fidget spinners. Was going to make a killing. Trouble was, they didn't spin.

Shit-storm.

I'm going to pay Oggy off for my old man, is no big deal.

The whole six grand? How are you going to…?

I have business interests of my own, Lis.

I knows you're a drug dealer, Marc Chapps. Everyone knows. Everyone knows you puts in tomato plants to make it look… it's like dressing a display of shit with Mars bars, you're not fooling no one.

Dealer is a bit harsh… we're in a cooperative.

I feel this makes it sound a lot more ethical than it is – sort of like the actual Co-op. In fact I felt disappointed and betrayed when it turned out the Co-op was just a bunch of shitholes like every other bank. When their chairman or whatever was exposed as some fat, whore-fucking cokehead it was as if the name of the FCC – Fairwater Cannabis Cooperative – had also been tarnished.

Part Three

By the way, before I go on I got to say that thing about me and Rachel Patterson at the party isn't true. I had sex with her and she enjoyed it very much. Right?

Any hint of sun and Vicci Park is a magnet for the new ones and the old ones.

Either in the splash pool or on a bench with an ice cream.

I settles on a bench – dedicated to Angela who, apparently, used to watch the world go by from here. Lisa comes back with the 'ice creams'.

A fucking Mini Milk – that's not an ice cream.

You want it or not?

The Mini Milk takes all of thirty seconds to eat.

You shops in New Look.

What you on about – ?

You still got the tag on your top. Sticking out the back.

I'm such a fucking idiot. Can you pull it off?

I leans into Lisa, so close I'm almost touching the little hairs on the back of her neck with my lips.

What you doing, Marc?

As my teeth close around the label I can't help but breathe through my nose down the back of her top.

Is the best way to get these things off – with your teeth.

As I pull at the tag it won't break and I'm starting to pull her hoodie against her neck and I'm thinking she must think I'm a right fucking maniac and then, thankfully, I feel the quick snap of the plastic tag – which I swallow.

Lisa is the type of girl who always looks good in any shit and also looks like the type of person who is always on the verge of telling you something.

She told me something: *Marc, you know when we was in school...*

Here we go.

Remember we went on that trip to Chessington World of Adventures? On the bus? We was like animals – all escaped for the day. We'd smuggled on all that cider and I was dying for a piss.

I can kinda remember but –

And I had to go and I was on the back seat and I was going to piss in a carrier bag and everyone was crowding round and they would have all watched but you made them turn around and you stood there, shielding me while I pissed in the bag.

You sure it was me?

When we got there I got off with David Swan.

–

I wish I'd gotten off with you. I was such a fucking idiot back then. Made some bad choices. Must admit I did have a bit of a crush on you.

I fucking knew it.

Took me ages to get over you.

Oh.

Then she hits me with the big whammy.

You ever been in love, Marc?

I waffles on for a few minutes – could have been an hour – about how I'm like an armadillo, all tough outside cos I don't want the inside getting bruised. I might have actually said armadildo.

Lisa got the hint and we did what Angela would have wanted us to do on her bench – watch the world go by.

I breaks the ice.

If you had some cash – some real cash – what would you do with it?

She thinks for moment – Lisa, not Angela, as Angela is obviously dead:

Oh I dunno, something boring, something everyone wants to do – maybe go to Spain and work hard in a proper bar and not worry about all this shit.

Life's no easier abroad, Lis – just cos the sun is shining don't make it better.

My mum always wanted to live somewhere sunny. What about you?

Curly fries.

What?

I always wants them but they're always more so I always goes for the normal ones – then regrets it. And a car. Not a shit one. An Audi. And a motorbike – Kawasaki. And a helicopter.

Any more forms of transport?

And a new house for my dad.

–

Is your mum still with us, Marc?

Yes. Unfortunately.

You don't see her?

Not if I can help it.

It's important. You only get one mum.

Thank fuck.

–

We get up and do some walking instead of talking.

Uh, this place should be famous. People should know about Victoria Park. He's famous. Sort of. Not famous famous. Cardiff famous.

What is that?

That's Billy the Seal. Captured forever in bronze.

A statue of a seal?

Lisa had been to Vicci Park many times with her mum – it's the type of place you'd push a person with a weird wasting disease around in a wheelchair – but no one had pointed out the life-size statue of the seal before.

How the fuck can you miss Billy?

'Billy the Seal, resident of Victoria Park lake from 1912 to 1939.' Well, I never.

He nearly escaped. Straight up. Was kept in this lake and there was this flood and he got out. He swam down Cowbridge Road and caught a tram towards the docks.

Good for you, Billy.

But.

There's always a 'but'.

He was this far from freedom – almost back in the sea… if he hadn't stopped for fish and chips and a pint of Brains Dark he would have made it to the ocean.

What happened to him? To Billy?

Brought him back. Spent the rest of his days here and he died of a broken heart. Never saw the sea again. My dad told me the story. We'd use to come here – as a family – and I'd spend hours with Billy, pretending we was on a ocean adventure together.

–

Rub his nose.

What?

If you rubs Billy's nose it brings you luck.

Fuck off.

Straight up, Lis.

Of course she had to do it.

She rubs it and I swear, the world goes a bit Matrix again – that ripple thing… ripples out around the park. Like a sonic boom, making everything liquid.

Rub-a-fucking-dub-dub.

Zooooooooooooooooop. Fucking weird.

Lisa is moving towards me and we're leaning in to each other and she tilts her head this way and I tilt my head that way and our lips are about to touch when…

There's a new character standing in line at the kiosk.

Oggy.

No minders, no Gary or Mo.

Just one of the crowd.

Wearing cargo pants and a T-shirt. Buying a 99.

He turns and seems like a nice, normal park-goer until he sees me and Lisa standing either side of Billy's bronze nose.

And he changes – a physical transformation.

More hunched but taller. More mean, more cruel.

But the problem is… He's still holding a 99.

Difficult to look gangsta when you're holding an ice cream.

With two Flakes in it.

Oggy saunters over, trying to hold the ice cream as if it was something only he could possess.

A nine-millimetre cone.

Looking at Lis, he says to me:

I hope you're not chatting up my girl, Wendy.

In fact, I was about to rub Billy's nose.

You getting lippy?

–

You know what, brah? I used to stare at this girl every day in reg class but she never gave me the time of day.

Well, fuck me, everyone was at it.

But now, I can buy her.

He gets in the space between Lisa and me and takes a lick of his Mr Whippy.

I am buying you, Lisa Short.

He takes a long, slow lick of his ice cream.

Sweet, yeah?

Impulse.

Again.

The air liquid, everything slow with the bass turned down real low…

The punch I deliver to the back of Oggy's head isn't that hard.

I remember thinking – like I was already spewing out my defence – it's not the punch that killed him, your honour, but the impact of Richard's frontal lobe with the metallic nose of the statue. It was Billy that killed him. I swears.

Oggy goes down like a sack of shit being dropped from a very great height.

Boompf.

Fuck.

Go, Marc.

Fuck.

Go, Marc.

My legs seemed to have stopped working.

There's a little river of blood coming from under Oggy's face and meandering to the bottom of Billy's plinth. His ice cream's still in his hand; he must have been really looking forward to that ice cream to get two Flakes.

Go, Marc.

I'm thinking – this is Lisa telling me to go but I looks up and sees it's Billy who's saying to me:

Go, Marc!

I look round and Gary and Mo are strolling through the park; they'd gone to park the car and it's fucking typical of Oggy he never thought to buy them ice cream.

Billy jumps down from his plinth and is heading for the bottom gate. He turns and waves a flipper at me.

For fuck's sake, Marc, run!

This time my legs obey Billy.

We run past the pool and the adventure bit and the flowerbeds and out the bottom gate and on to Cowbridge Road East and left and towards town and past the Clive and Tesco and over the crossroads and past the Jobcentre and the cheap fruit shop and the Co-op – the fucking Co-op – and Iceland and into Canton, avoiding shoppers and prams and past Cash Converters and only as we get to the Westgate do we catch our breath. Billy's leaning a flipper against the door to the boarded-up pub.

Right.

Says Billy.

What are our options: catch a Stagecoach to the Brecon Beacons, train to Carmarthen, maybe Stannie can help you… Where you going, Marc?

I'm not like you, Billy.

I know that – I'm a fucking seal.

I'm a killer on the run – but if I'm going, I'm going for good.

*The bus station is this way. Marc? I been on that plinth for
a hundred years thinking about getting out of that fucking park
and, trust me, this is not how you escape.*

But you got caught. Why should I trust you?

If you can't trust a talking seal, Marc, who can you trust?

*Of all the 'killer-on-the-run' movies I've seen they all needs one
thing to escape – cash.*

–

Cyncoed.

Posh as fuck.

By the time we got to Hollybush Road I was knackered.

Opposite the bay-window-fronted, high-gated, four-bedroom
semi, I sat on a low wall and checked my lungs were still in
my chest.

I soaked the sweat into my T-shirt and tried to calm my shaking
hands and legs.

I looks around for Billy but he's nowhere in sight.

The doorbell plays some sort of classical music. The door –
which seemed bigger than a normal door – opens.

She was dressed like she was going to a cocktail party: in lime-
green with matching green shoes and what I think is called a
fascinator in her hair.

I need to come in, Celia.

I couldn't help but stare at the thing perched in her hair.

You practising for Ascot?

Are you okay, Marc?

She was in the middle of a phone conversation:

I'll call you back, my son has just popped in.

'Popped in'! We hadn't seen each other in the best part of
three years.

You alone? I make the question into an accusation.

Yes, I'm alone.

—

I been alone for the past couple of years.

I've nothing cutting or generous to say to that and I don't want to ask but I do:

Where's…?

Simon?

I'd forgotten Bunce had a first name.

We split up a little while ago…

I'd often wondered whether Celia knew about Bunce's men beating up the old man – had she even encouraged it or was it the reason they split up? I'd never asked, or was likely to ask, about it. I'd also never asked if the old man had stolen the doors cos he knew they were Bunce's.

You want something to drink?

I had a lemonade which I instantly regretted – wishing I'd had something a bit more grown-up.

You in trouble, Marc?

I wants to say: well, yeah, I just killed a man and the police are looking for me, I'm part of a drugs cartel which every fucker seems to know about and my sidekick is a seal but apart from that everything's tip-top. But it's…

I needs cash and I needs it now.

What happened next was like a scene from one of those black-and-white movies.

Celia gets up, straightens her fascinator, walks to the side of the room and unhooks a French-looking painting of a girl picking flowers to reveal a safe.

I get up and look out the back window as I hear click that way, click, back again, click, and I considers telling Celia she's got a seal in her swimming pool but think better of it. Billy waves at me. I don't wave back.

I pick up a copy of this month's issue of Global Event Management magazine which, if I had flicked through, featured my old girl in a small article with a head-and-shoulders piccy on page thirty-nine. Below, on the table, is a letter from Cardiff and Vale Health Board – oncology unit. I drop the magazine back down like a lead weight.

Click this way and clunk.

Celia sits and counts out the cash, laying it on the coffee table.

As the girl in the painting would have said: Voilà.

There's six thousand pounds, Marc.

You're kidding me – six grand?

To the penny. It's all I've got.

Six grand – fucking weird… but no time to think about that now.

As I reached forward for the cash the merest hint of a look from Celia stops me from touching it.

At the end of the day, I'm your mother, Marc. You frustrate the hell out of me but I love you, you know that, don't you? Take the cash – but there is a condition, Marc.

Of course there is.

This is a loan. If you fail to pay this back within a month then you have to come and live with me. Here. And leave all that… other stuff behind. My house means my rules. Understand?

So that's what you wants?

Marc?

I shifts the magazine and holds the letter.

You wants me to be some kind of fucking nursemaid?

Don't need one. I'm with BUPA. I only wants the best for my boy, is that too much to ask? You going to take the cash or not?

Part Four

Okay, so where we going? Rio? India?

Slow down, Billy, I got some time before…

Come on, Marc, you got to get out of Cardiff now.

I can't leave without saying goodbye…

Saying goodbye?! Don't be like me, Marc – I was caught, we've got the cash, let's go – you know it's the right thing to do. What are you doing now? You checking train times?

Me and Billy get an Uber back to Fairwater. We sit in silence. As the car pulls into the car park, Billy flops a flipper on to my arm and looks up at me with those big stupid eyes of his:

You're going to get caught, Marc.

The clock reads four-oh-seven as I enter the Ex. My old man is in his favourite corner with a pint of SA and a book. Half of him in Fairwater with the afternoon drinkers and half of him in Barbados with Bond.

Want a drink, son?

No, I, uh… I've come to say I'm going away for a bit. A holiday.

I puts two of the six grand on the table.

For you.

He lays James Bond face down, shielding 007 from this crime.

I don't want to explain too much but…

He leans into me, the smell of Brains SA on his breath.

Give me some credit, son. I'm not saying I don't need this money, not saying I don't want it but, believe me, I can't take it. Would you? I can handle Oggy.

This isn't for Oggy, you don't have to worry about him – this is for you.

Thanks but no thanks. You sure you don't want a pint, son? My shout. Sue behind the bar said you was in here earlier – with a girl who was drinking fizzy wine. That who you're going on holiday with?

Uh, no. I'm going with, well, it's complicated.

Shame. Sue said you made a smashing couple. She said you seemed... at ease with each other.

Did she...?

–

Promise me, son, you'll give that money back, wherever it came from. Yeah?

At that point all I want to do is have a pint with my old man in the comfortable and familiar surroundings of the Ex.

Sorry, Mark, got to go.

You promise?

I promise.

Happy days, son. Don't worry about me. Fizzy wine!

The old man takes a sip of his SA and plunges back into 007's battle to bring some justice to this crappy world.

Outside, Billy is balancing an empty can of Red Bull on his nose.

You all done now, Marc? Can you drive? Should we hire a car and go to France? Marc? Marc, where you going?

–

I sees her go up the front path and into the house.

It's a shock for her as she tries to close the door – my hand is stopping it.

Can I come in?

She walks through to the kitchen and I follow.

I was going to do a runner and then I saw my dad and he said something to me and I thought…

What did he say?

I haven't got long, the police will be looking for me, but he said, well someone else said and he repeated it –

What did he say?

He said: we make a smashing couple.

Lisa moves a tiny bit closer to me and I'm starting to well up and she's starting to well up:

If I stay in Fairwater I'm going to die of a broken heart.

–

Let's fuck off together, Lis, let's go away with this…

–

I got six grand and we can start again, just me and you. Isn't that a brilliant idea? Leave Fairwater.

Where'd you get it? The money.

–

Where, Marc?

That don't matter.

Sorry, it does.

I might not even have to pay it back, depending.

Depending on what?

BUPA:

She shifts to her left, facing me.

You're in love with me, Marc Chapps. Always was, ever since we was in reg class.

You got it the wrong way round – you was in love with me.

Marc Chapps loves Lisa Short.

*No, no, I just wants to fuck you. Tha's all. I wants to buy you
just like Oggy was going to buy you. I wants you to be my
sugar baby.*

I can see she don't believe me and I can see I'm in trouble. Big
fucking trouble.

She moves towards me.

We don't have to run away, Marc, to be together.

Now she's closer and there's no need for either of us to say
anything.

I'm unaware of who's moving forward; could be me, could be
her. Or maybe the world is getting that little bit smaller each
millisecond and we're both riding an ever-shrinking brown-and-
white Ikea rug towards each other until we are this far apart.

And we kiss.

Oh yes, we kiss. How we kiss.

Boom.

My world expands a little and different points on our bodies are
making connections

And we kiss. Again. This time it's all me and she pulls away a bit
and I grab hold of her and bring her to me – she's like a fucking
yo-yo at this point.

Her lips are tickling the little hairs on my earlobe as she
whispers something to me and I'm so out of it that I don't catch
what she says and the focus of her watery eyes shifts away from
mine and I turn and I realise why she whispered 'you have to
get out of here now'.

Oggy stands in the doorway to the kitchen. Gary and Mo stand
behind him.

Oggy is not dead.

Oggy, you're not dead, thank fuck for that!

I rush forward and hug him and then realise this is, in the
circumstances, highly inappropriate.

I stand back and notice Oggy's head has a massive bandage around it. Both his eyes are black. The missing front tooth makes him look harder than he is.

Yeah, that's right, brah, I'm not dead.

I don't feel as though he's about to call me Wendy or tell the story about us at Rachel Patterson's party.

Which, I have to emphasise, again, is not true.

Look, Oggy, I'm sorry, just an accident, yeah? Here, you can have this six thousand pounds, it'll clear Lisa's debt, yeah? We're all mates, yeah? Brah…?

He shakes his pinhead of a head.

I know there's no getting out of this – this is how it happens in gangster movies: Oggy is going to kill me. I can't fight back cos if I do Gary and Mo will get involved. I can predict every move Oggy will make. I've known him and his type all my life and I knows what he will do next. He'll take a step forward.

Oggy takes a step forward.

He will get out some sort of weapon to beat me with.

It's half a pool cue. The bottom half.

I'm begging you, Oggy, please. Let us both go.

Kiss my trainers.

What?

Lick the Nike. Just do it.

The tip of my tongue licks the tick.

Please, Oggy. Please…

He slowly unbuttons his cargo pants and out flops his cock.

Now give little Oggy a little kiss.

He's going to make me suck him off, then he's going to kill me.

I turn to Gary and Mo. They look away, this is too much even for them.

Come on, Marky, little Oggy wants kisses.

And what happens if I do give, uh, little Oggy kisses?

You can walk out of here alive. Well, you might not be walking but... What you crying for, Marc? Come on, what you waiting for?

And she does it.

Lisa stabs Oggy in the ribs – he stops, a dramatic pause if ever there was one.

From where I'm kneeling I can see it's a big knife, with a big black handle. Something you might use for chopping larger veg.

The knife sinks into a point in the middle of Oggy's gut. It thrust up and sideways and split the stomach lining in two, cutting a slice off Oggy's left lung before puncturing his heart. Surprisingly there wasn't much blood to start with. That soon changed though.

This time he doesn't go down like a sack of shit. Lisa steps back and Oggy brings down the pool cue, drops it, it clatters, he staggers forward and leans on the kitchen table, cock still out. For a second looks he like he's just taking a rest.

Then he goes down like a sack of shit.

I looks down and Beyoncé is looking back up at me – she ain't moving.

Oh oh oh. Oh oh oh.

The coroner later said the blade, measuring five-point-four inches long, was probably purchased from Argos.

We snap back to real time and Gary and Mo are already out the house.

While Lisa's being sick in the sink I turns and sees Billy out the kitchen window. He gives me a wink and runs down Fairwater Road as fast as his flippers can take him.

Epilogue

Celia's considering her options: she's down to some lobster thing or oysters. The restaurant isn't posh posh but it isn't Fairwater Fish Bar; put it like this – I'm the only one wearing white socks.

The old girl nearly wet herself when I suggested a holiday.

Yeah, before this cancer thing – before they starts cutting lumps out of you.

Just a minor operation, Marc, nothing for you to worry about.

Who said I was fucking worried, Celia?

Mind your language, Marc. My house, my rules. Where should we go?

I was thinking about Switzerland –

Switzerland? Why?

But maybe somewhere warmer might be better.

I was hating it – I particularly hate sand. And with Marbella being on the coast there's no getting away from the sand. At least Celia was paying.

As Celia considers the menu, it strikes me that she couldn't have sanctioned Bunce's men beating the shit out of the old man – I've learnt she hates any type of violence. Except to shellfish, obviously.

I could see Celia was in the mood to share – and I'm not talking tapas.

Tell me, Marc.

Tell you what, Celia?

Anything you like, love. I've got three years of Marc to catch up on.

When you and the old man split up I didn't understand it – first thing I thought was, could I have stopped them? After a while I thought everything was your fault. Now, I can see things are more grey than black and white.

I told her about drug dealing, living in Fairwater, about Oggy, about the cops turning up to a house in Fairwater to find him dead with his cock out and half a pool cue shoved up his arse.

I shared with her the scene after Lisa had stabbed Oggy – of the holdall I packed for her, the warm cash in fifty-quid notes I placed in the side-zipped pocket along with a Dove deodorant and a bar of soap (at that moment I remember thinking how refreshing it was that Lisa used soap and not shower gel), the frantic phone call to Stannie:

I needs a big favour, Stannie, one you'll actually have to get out the house for.

I told her about Lisa, in a stupor, being led out the door, of her getting into a Vauxhall Astra.

When it was her turn, Celia shared a story of when her and the old man had sex in a hedge. I know.

The waitress walks towards our table and I can see that she does look good in anything and I remember having that very same thought at Cantonian High School, even though she sat behind me.

Hi, my name is Wendy, you ready to order?

I'll have the lobster linguine and a glass of Rioja and my son will have…

Curly fries and a pint of cava.

Lisa laughs.

I laugh.

Celia gives an embarrassed shake of her head as Lisa returns to the bar.

I can see the sea from where we're sat. It looks fantastic.

I sit there, waiting for my fizzy wine, glad that I'm not on my own, concentrating on the waves as they gently wash away what's gone before.

In the surf I see a head bobbing along. Not the head of a swimmer but... it's Billy. Of course it fucking is. He lies on his back, flippers in the air, basking in the sun. He lifts his flipper and gives me a little wave before disappearing, diving deeper into the sea.

The End.

Other Titles in this Series

A Nick Hern Book

Sugar Baby first published in Great Britain in 2017 as a paperback original by Nick Hern Books Limited, The Glasshouse, 49a Goldhawk Road, London W12 8QP, in association with Dirty Protest

Reprinted 2018

Sugar Baby copyright © 2017 Alan Harris

Alan Harris has asserted his right to be identified as the author of this work

Cover illustration by Nic Finch

Designed and typeset by Nick Hern Books, London
Printed in the UK by Mimeo Ltd, Huntingdon, Cambridgeshire PE29 6XX

A CIP catalogue record for this book is available from the British Library

ISBN 978 1 84842 674 0

Woodland CARBON
www.woodlandcarbon.co.uk
NICK HERN BOOKS
Printed on Carbon Captured paper